Devils Tower

I0177785

m otis aavenüe

Compiled and produced by microdot media | Unalaska, AK 99692
A Matt Reinders Proprietary Business

Please address inquires to

    Devils Tower

    microdot media. http://www.poetryinprint.com/

    otis.aavenue@gmail.com

Library of Congress Cataloging-in-Publication Data

Library of Congress Control Number: 2011961380

ISBN-978-0-9848553-2-2

    1. poetry-general

page count: 52

Manufactured in the United States of America

Thanks to:

Rick Robbins, Terry Davis, Cathy Day, Ed Micus & Roger Schaeffer

Roberto, The Reverend Denver K, Henry Jones, LorioQ,
the Crawzack-Kummrow team,

TJ Foster, Bill the Cowboy Poet and rest of the Klamathites,
Blue Skunks, poverty, all the Gutterkings, the Guttaspankas and
general troublemakers in WDC – Starlite Lanes –

Lärs Erikson, Duggan,
Minnesota,
ma, pa and the support of family and friends.

No one knows where m otis aavenüe disappeared in the Sonoran Desert or how he may have passed. Only his glass eye remained trapped under a Manzanita bush. Evidence suggested he was consumed by a mountain lion. Family and friends believe he died practicing a lifestyle he loved. Others have created a legend that he was discovered by Chupacabra while sleeping under the stars, while some still speculate he illegally crossed the boarder into Mexico and continued on a path toward Argentina. We may never discover all the facts.

We do know he was hiking across America in search of the raw truth of his life and inspiration for a non-fiction book about combining living in poverty with practicing deep ecology. We also know he left many of his unpublished and unfinished works with his close friend, publisher and property manager, Matthew Reinders, who continues to be his best advocate and ally.

Microdot Media is now proud to publish m otis aavenüe's work. Devils Tower was the first of his many unpublished chapbooks. We have worked diligently to preserve the original formats, however have also taken liberty to edit and produce his craft of the written word so that his restless and free spirit may live on.

Thanks You.

Devils Tower

m otis aavenüe

CONTENTS

The West Was Somewhere Under All Those gray Clouds In 1999

Route 66 In The Rain

Driving Through The Ozarks At Night
        With A Friend Once Thought To Be Dead

Epitaph Of The Midwestern Plains Drifter

After The Runway Approach At Minneapolis International Airport

Leaving The Platinos Club At Eight PM With A Prostitute

Kicking Booze At The Village Of Shells

Watching The Tide Come In From A Fishing Boat
        With Roberto Cedillos Mata

Living With A Mexican Wristwatch

We Dance With Men At The Beach Of Carmen

With Five Ranch Hands Remembering The Klamath

Turning Sixty In Another's Spring

Reborn at Riverfront Park

. . .walk to the rhythm of breathing – inhale,
     exhale, like wind that smashes hedgerow ash –
imagine indigenous iambic –
     echoes of Mississippian nomads
gathering clam and wild rice eons past –
     their milling stones like your grinding molars.
Focus eyes on swirling silt and sewage
     stirred into the Minnesota River
by the undertow of state highway bridge
     pilings choked to the riprap with driftwood.
Imagine station wagon caravans
     of families drive overhead like flocks
of sparrows – forget the first spring you met
     the love you thought would last karmic lifetimes.
She mentioned breaking into broken homes,
     nihilist hate of parents, family and friends –
tears ran to her chin when her stepsister
     left for boarding school, left alone to learn
about fellatio from twenty-four-
     year-old methamphetamine producers –
until meeting you – realizing your search –
     for people gazing moonlit horizons,
or visit cities to ride public trains
     downtown to collect character portraits
and provide what you could never possess
     but often thought you would like to borrow.

*   *   *

Robins hopscotch along the granite bed
of a rail line. Paint chips flake in layers
and fall
from my bathroom window as it opens.
I breathe deep through my nose to smell winter's
work of decomposed leaves like urine soaked
among the silent mounds in the latrine –
dandelion pollen stings nose, throat, eyes.
Return to bed! Sleep off this hangover.

She smiles – eyes closed, face undone, guard let down –
like shaped marble wrapped in soft silk bedsheets.
Dreaming again, hand over hand, they waltz
across the floor, beyond the window glass
down a flight of Lilac bush, over the
duck pond, past graffiti tagged nuclear
cooling towers, into one three-hundred
acre diesel train and boxcar graveyard
where they drop down open storm drains, alone.

Every city grows grassy stone skin over
PVC circulatory systems
pumping, flushing, water, sewer, storm-waste –
a catacomb of pipes – art studio –
autoerotic asphyxiation –
mold masturbation mannequin fetish –
a loss-less copper figure for hot lead
or jaundice watercolor plastic cream.

The neighbor's Pit Bull yo-yos on her chain.
Her master adjusts his loose, dry glass eye
and fumbles for his cardboard grocery bag.
Eggshells burst on limestone – ooze almost life.
His dog laps fertile ground – tongue like pink sponge.
They whine together – mourning together.

> *   *   *

I remember my molars chiseled | chewed
      by cement | mixed with ant dirt and mortar –
punched out by a cold concrete stairway step –
      like stained porcelain on stained porcelain
the teeth in a bathtub spotted with blood.

> *   *   *

Now noon, on a Sunday, she bends back
like a short hair tabby – head on my lap.
From this bed in our one room apartment
we look down
        on the uptown traffic jammed
in confused commute. I light opium
incense sticks and know she will pick an ear
scab until it bleeds and I tell her stop.
It is time again to walk in the park. . .

Twenty-First Birthday in the Wet Lands

#1

I shoplift a pint of Southern Comfort
and hike the train tracks into the country
to breathe corn pollen
         and the old oak leaves.
The mosquito, a blood hungry glutton –
as all nature is – feeds off my fare skin.
They curse me like recurring night terrors
– dreams cut down and slaughtered – stuffed in old boots –
to keep away from smell, taste or touch.
My hometown has never felt so empty.
I have lost myself with purpose this time.

#2

If I could shrink to explore the carpet
of my bedroom – searching the shadows –
and live among the mites who reside there;
then I would be small and have weightless limbs.
I could look out and gain new perspective
on the people and places I come from.
Outside my broken window a half-moon sinks
behind clouds. I study the chalky face
and think it studies me among the mites.

#3

I ogle tits blurred blue through reflection
as they waltz behind a Methodist Church
stained glass window and imagine the bride's
mother as a turtle neck lesbian
– corduroy capri pants long on short legs –
her eyes faint nipples behind dark glasses.
Together we chant serenity prayers
and carry Christ with us after his death –
sleep – sink – to the bottom of the wet lands.

Geometry Of Men And Women

Lightning bugs
blink along rectangle beds of roses
      silhouettes of oak
      bathe in moon-bleached shadow.

I deconstruct the conversation
we had between sips of Sumatran coffee
      between subtle glances
      sincere as puppy awe –

my equilateral skull
cocked in acute angle.

Parallel as reflections in water
I felt with you then
      we hugged like conjoined twins
      in the same plaid pajamas –

symmetrical
in point-of-view and unable to part
      from comparing failed love
      to failed love.

People of our pasts
fell like baby teeth from gums
    Euclidean smiles
    webbed across faces.

I could have kissed
the perpendicular nap at the base of your nose
    the Roman Arches
    above your eyes.

Instead
I offer to refill your empty cup
    and we rotate away
    through proved equations.

What Have We Had Apart From Fragmented Lives

Sweating the seconds of a sales clerk's smile,
a bellhop holding your attache case,
by chance we meet, hug between gulps of stout
like jellyfish groping the hotel bar –
too drunk to stand still. I drop my glass mug.
Your leather mitts shake my velvet horse jaw
and bring a new beer.

                    I chewed you in dreams
for four weeks – in Paris, Machu Picchu,
Peking, Prague – you only knew in crayon
letters scribbled along brick bathroom walls.
I could only think of limericks then,
and now cannot forget –

                    Dictionary
    pages as thoughts   stumble
              white legged between
    chicken screen sanitarium walls and
    eyes   stare from eyes paper
              mache bleached
    sift dreams like rims spin on a wheel-
              chair
    thirteen screams from personalities
              end
              of a lecture hall. We bob opposite
shores across oceans of smoke and brown ash,
apart,
         between mountains of animal-
skinned people. You listen, roll marble eyes
along the ceiling, chewing plastic pen
like rock candy, while geology text
erupts from a professor that points to
French Guiana. I flee like Papillon
to the men's room, dodging staff and students.
Fist-in-hand, we should have left together.

Alone,
        forehead to forehead with mirror
above a porcelain sink, I run water
over chalked knuckles, baptize chin and neck –
we are not orange monarch butterflies.
We are not acres of blue grass or corn –
together, we are air in a lightbulb.

Falling In Lust With A Cocktail Waitress

Eyes like mandarin orange garnishes,
her onyx pupils refract through the brim
of my wineglass
and I foam at the mouth
like the Colorado River's – no smiles –
only fists of own hair under neon.

        Pablo's Blue Guitarist burns on easel
        half-buried in Arizona Sand   Dust
        devils vault Grand Canyon walls
        spill over
        High Sierras
        filter through citrus trees
        and ageless sequoias   this potent wind
        poisonous as acid rain
        desert dry
        sloughs redwood's bark like virgin confessions –
        pours
        xenophile   chlorophyl
        blastocyst   vacuole
        ribosomes   23rd chromosomes

I split my face, ear
to ear, with a knife.

Habits Of A Traveling Arsonist

He listens to telephone rings and lights his sixteenth Lucky Strike,
lets yellow butane flame gutter, french curves bent on hotel curtains
in DC-12 exhaust before television-gray screen, static
and toilet water have ran for three hours – he waits in white noise
for her to call. That's a hundred dollars, honey, blows in left ear.

"I do," his wife says through a white veil.
Her eyes like sharp green emeralds.
He remembers her blinking razor thin lashes, pastor's chapped lips
tasting geraniums in his breath, hearing himself speak in tongues.
"I do," he agrees, wilts arms like lilies, tucks hair behind right ear.

Outside the open Marriott window, off Snelling Avenue,
taxi honks like a waiting wedding limousine and he watches
white nylon tear on his hooker's sandpaper calf. My life, he thinks,
pennies in a wishing well. He bathes in Bacardi one-five-one
and sets his bed on fire.

Finally – Seeing Myself Behind The Reflection In Glass

We hold hands on a stone bench, watched by glass
eyes of ceramic toads flashing between
rose petals under the sun – in minutes
the sky will swell gray with clouds – no rainbows
run like shooting stars above our blue house.
Our neighbors lock kids inside the brick fence
of their yard behind green garage, its van
smokes with exhaust. I wait for us to cry
like skinned children, but the tears never come.
Particleboard bloats in a porcelain
pan on broken steps of our porch. Laughter
rains under the thunder of lawn mowers.
Next door, chicken roasts on a grill – seconds
before they fight like cocks in a dirt pen
for the last time today.
                    I hold the air
with white knuckles where our hands used to rest
on concrete – sandpaper in sandpaper –
she complained of ulcers, joked she's pregnant
without us meeting green eyes to green eyes.
We sat for hours wishing like school-brat-
middle-aged parents for successful sons,
successful daughters; for children to grow
away from living like rocks in mortar.
We sat lifeless as a conjoint frog,
stomach up, preserved in formaldehyde.

Fishing For The End Of A Marriage

We snag one another with silver hooks
downrigging in iceberg-cocktail waters
of a Minneapolis bar. Her moon
face breaks the Uptown's pavement horizon,
pale as night's dawn. My gray, plastic devil
mask stares from black holes across quartz fishponds
of smoke. No one notices our nonsmiles.
I straighten yellow butterfly collars,
blink bullhead eyes in jaundice nebula
of bottom feeding, and she – fragmented –
in the crystal hexagons of my gin
glass, drifts through the kaleidoscope doorway.

Walking Past Denesen's Warehouse
To The Grocery Store On Lake Street

Semi trailers rise – Aztec pyramids –
from Yucatan jungles of twisted elm
and iron. A broken Denesen's sign
leans from the road on a cowering fence,
rusted syllables on separate planes
of weed eaten wood.
                        Across Colfax Street,
the warehouse wears shutters around windows
like a mechanic's lapels at a wake.
White brick mourns for Bungor, HK, Otis –
bruised red and blue through graffiti warfare.
Three mixed youth spark a joint on Twenty-eighth.
I march along the bridge, over railroad
tracks bent in rising heat.
                        A naked man
toggles left and right against the bronze line,
a leather tanned handcar in slow motion,
shaved head glowing white-hot, reflects sun.
He disappears in a mushroom of dust,
and I, into the doors of a grocery store.

Driving Through Iowa With Lars Erikson

Pillars of sun hold clouds above silver
hog barns along Interstate 35.
The ditch flows in grass
waves past the window.
We listen to Al Green's *Here I Am*, drink
water from plastic jugs and imagine
our lives as heroin junkies on skids
from Wall Street 8-balls,
sharkskin suits and silk
ties that hang from smiles lined with pearls.
      A deer
drapes the shoulder of highway – its stomach
stuffed with two days of death like a balloon
about to burst. I pet
my beard and have dreamed enough for one day.

Having Breakfast May 9 In A Broomfield Townhouse

Snowflakes like dandruff
    on black birds
around bronze fountains
    in the yard.
The temperature dropped
    two degrees
to twelve Celsius.

    A gray tom
in the neighbor's porch
    paws its glass
door with steam pistons
    of its fur
locomotive. The
    birds blink eyes
lazy as cows' and
    black as my
Sumatran coffee.

The West Was Somewhere Under All Those gray Clouds
In 1999

'76 New Yorker jolts to a stop at Texaco
in Ovid, Colorado. A man in khakis starts fuel pump
to feed his thirty gallon tank, careful with hose near a duct
taped bumper that hangs six inches from gray pavement.
                This Atlas
under Earth's weight in car-top carrier, flaunts Barbies in rear
windshield like tacky plastic jewelry.
                Four daughters scratch like cats
at the doors and pour out to stretch their legs.
                He turns oatmeal face
south, leans on the trunk to let wind blow through his comb
                over – squints
toward foothills, lets eyes glaze in gas fumes. Yucca
lines the western horizon like a sultan's crown.
He lifts the youngest to his shoulder
and points as she stares pony-eyed into sun.

Through a cloud of cigarette smoke
I look out a hotel window,
glasses slide off my greasy nose,
and watch an American flag
lick wind. Constant hum of semi
traffic fills the room while I drink
away a hangover with gin
and peel layers of nicotine
yellow wallpaper from under
the air-conditioner. I want
to call the US president
on the touch tone phone – my elbows
on plastic wood grain tabletop –
ask if Eisenhower's highways
will outlast China's Great Wall or
topple like the wall in Berlin.

Route 66 In The Rain

Over a no parking sign
painted yellow on black tar
a calico cat with mange
limps through a puddle – pregnant –
but rain pours down anyway.
Smells of burned leaves and auto
tires hang, incense smoke in air.
Flagstaff is a motel town
with discount food chains, pay phones
and RV parks crippled drunks
return to, spilling coffee
from both fists after stealing
cups at Days Inn blocks ago.
Vacant lots swallowed in weeds
like old cemeteries sick
with neglect stop at sidewalk's
edge – shopping carts, cups and cans
flow along the square cement
into a flooded ravine.
"Flagstaff" scribbled on cardboard –
a hitchhiker's sign. Across
the street at Safeway Grocery,
college girls call like turkeys
under a dripping awning.
Their arms swing like pendulums
with the weight of tomatoed

soups in stretching plastic bags.
Gunplay echoes down alley
and the bank clock a half block
away displays one minute
before three thirty AM.
I walk home past the burned couch
on a warehouse dock behind
trailer chimneys that puff wood
smoke humble as corncob pipes.
From the shadows a father
shoulders his son who giggles
when they bump down the gutter
on a squeaking mountain bike.

Driving Through The Ozarks At Night
With A Friend Once Thought To Be Dead

Crickets consume the neighborhood
    with buzzes loud as transistors.

Behind his rock quarried shoulders
    vacant lots of dead grass shift like tide,
and he lifts his steam shovel head,
    mastodon slow, to scrape answers
        from Springfield's limestone layered cliffs.

Cowlicks of brown bushes and shrub
    on red hills wear the smell of skunks.

The night's humid air reminds me
    I am six hundred miles from bed
        and battle fatigues with no bus
            ticket, address or phone number.

Embedded along the highway
    in concrete, all the smooth pebbles
        point northward to Minnesota.

The dead face of the moon rises,
    rises on tails of falling stars
        behind lazy sagging cable
            between house and empty white house.

Together we careen over

      broken streets, past construction signs

            half shadowed as charcoal sketches

                  in a closing book – his moon face

Jesus hung in the driver's seat –

      mine like a hydrogen zeppelin

            torpedoed through inches of space

                to collide with the lunar cheek.

I turn, eye to eye, with the black

      planet of my thin reflection

            in the passenger side window.

He states I was as good a friend

      as a friend ever expected.

Epitaph Of The Midwestern Plains Drifter

The sky in Southern Minnesota
        speaks regional dialect at night.
Mosquitoes buzz in ears
        between drags off generic cigarettes.
Wagon trains of breath and smoke,
        pushed with corn silk lungs
after gins and tonics,
        sink in humid air.
Imagine life as the Seven Sisters
        staring, burning in Indian ink black midnight
– I, hydrogen hot, hope to burn half as bright
        – will sleep no more
until among them with pulsars'
        beats between rushes of blood
– will eat no more until spinning
        like an atomic top
and spitting solar wind at the sun
        – will shout no more in Spanish,
broken English or Iroquois,
        but speak softer than western wind
and everlasting as starlight.

After The Runway
   Approach At Minneapolis International Airport

Highway 55's banks of bare earth blur
past the bent lens of a Boeing window,
brown as oil stains on the gray concrete
beneath chrome tipped wings and engine exhaust.

I could have died in cold Minnesota –
saying good-bye to a lake-eyed mother,
or behind the wheel of a one-hundred-
mile-per-hour-once-rolled-already-and-
rebuilt-since-nineteen-sixty-eight-classic-
Pontiac-Ventura, bent on vodka,
or leaving the comfortable guiding grins
behind open arms, or could have passed
on precise as a pendulum in time
with hands like weathered wood around a hog's
pen – but did not.

   Jets wheeze and whine and suck
air. Mosaic of rust and blue on door
of hanger reminds me of the Koch pipes
twisted like oil refinery sized
sugar cubes gray as a pile of tires
– elements yielding to elements – a
metallic cat that arches back on shins
of humanity and screams for a scratch

behind wire brush ears. I stretch my legs.
The plane lifts off and interstate traffic,
falling hundreds of feet away from me,
has continued all-day, and it still will
continue tomorrow.

      I paid strangers
to hurl my body, with one-hundred and
two foreign peoples' around me, over
concrete cloverleaves, pillbox apartments,
pox marks of hardwood forest and river
mud that holds our farmyards of history.
In minutes, Nebraska looks like a loomed
quilt. This is the closest I will ever be
to becoming an astronaut, and last
time I will be with my America.

Leaving The Platinos Club At Eight PM With A Prostitute

A bulldozer of lumbering muscle,
I push cobbles along the dirt sidewalk –
drunker than twelve American tourists,
biceps tense like mariachi guitar
strings and too tired to wrestle around
Juanita's waist. Arm hair erect and my
nursing shark's jaw open, teeth Yucatan
dense, I feel focused as the calico
arching back to strike tortilla nibbling
mice under gray shadows of concrete piles
in the alley. Rodents explode to sprints
while a cinder block sun sinks between space
and pink horizon. Even the feline
is weak under a Mexican sunset –
her kinked tail still jerking, she wipes exhaust
from her face, those eyes deep and moody blue
as the black lights in her Platinos Club.

Kicking Booze At The Village Of Shells

IT HURTS TO SOBER
UNDER TROPICAL
SUN. EVERY DOG
BARK ECHOES LIKE FIRE
ALARMS. MY HEAD, VICED
BETWEEN CUPPED HAMMOCK,
SWINGS ON EASTERN WIND.
DEAD PALM LEAVES TUMBLE
ACROSS A MARBLE
FLOOR. FACE TO GECKO
FACE – CATATONIC –
THIS LIZARD IN LIME
TREE I WATCH, FROZEN,
IGNORING DC-
12 STOMACH AND CRACK
ANOTHER BOTTLE
OF WARM MODELO.

Watching The Tide Come In From A Fishing Boat
With Roberto Cedillos Mata

Napalm explodes behind my lazy
      eyelids
as sun lifts like an atomic bottle-rocket
over the Cozumel harbor.
Since I last slept, it's been a leap year
and a bobbing sailboat
      on the octopus ink horizon –
water, too dark to see through –
reminds me of my life.

Roberto pulls a Dorado into our anchored boat.
Its blue gills suck dry air, twenty peso coins
for eyes. He grins ear to ear.

We beg the sea to dwarf us,
to surround and consume our
      bones
like oil boils pink muscle to white meat.
We beg the dark water to swell and push us in orbit
between thin clouds. Then we'd look down
and pluck the black corals,
black pearls
and black reflections from Caribbean waves.

Living With A Mexican Wristwatch

Three-legged dog ruts nose through grocery bags
of spotted bananas and pollo bones
in the gutter of Juarez Street – whining,
dodges taxis, hops along the crosswalk
on piñata legs. Roberto's daughter
points her gold finger and watches with sun
stoned eyes. He scoops her to shoulders, tells me
tomorrow I fix el baño – his smile,
soft as a Gulf Breeze breaking sky blue waves.
The crests roll over themselves, sound like slow
moving locomotives with endless steam –
usch, usch – water recedes from crystal shore
and erodes the windblown veins from white sand.

We Dance With Men At The Beach Of Carmen

I
Five foot waves tall as a Mexican cigar
salesman burst like gray smoke from the mouth
of a pink coral reef. His sea salty eyes
linger behind brown crescents – her breasts
under shells of submarine nylon, shells
small as turtles', and she giggles
at his tobacco gold smile.

II
The father peddles his bicycle,
305 piston for a leg,
his son's leg a matchstick
in comparison, pushes the opposite crank
up and down to make the three wheeled bike
roll and roll over broken Juarez.
Buenos noches, his father shouts, fingers
folded around the clear neck of a Sol bottle.
The boy smiles.
They pump in unison as one machine.

III

Together, two palm trees
stand alone in the Yucatan forest.

IV

With my last dollar, I buy a pack of Boots
cigarettes for a friend in Minnesota.
A Mexican boy, maybe sixteen, slides orange
soda under his t-shirt and smiles as I watch,
drooling curiosity from my pale face.
I am not like him – opal eyes,
my sand-wet hair, white teeth and bubblegum
breath – we are the same. I squat in the street
to pat a brooding mutt that licks the air,
open the cigarettes, smoke, then smile
at the boy and walk into the alley.

With Five Ranch Hands Remembering The Klamath

One

Wind blows like cedar
sway between marble valleys.
The rocks sweat water.
       Tenements of moss
       rent rooms to banana slugs
       while the grasses die –
             their blades, piss yellow.
             I feel like grass in the sun
             and smile regardless.

With Five Ranch Hands Remembering The Klamath

Two

I picked a flower –
this center of all things – held
it with one finger –
> could have crushed the stem
> with dull botany tweezers
> and shaking gray hands –
> > it was fragile life,
> > and along the steep hillside
> > thousands covered earth.

With Five Ranch Hands Remembering The Klamath

Three

The half cratered gulch
like a bitten green apple
cups Spring's melting snow.
   Our pregnant cattle
   croon for the mountain meadows
   remembered as calves.
     I twist my mustache,
     throw coffee grounds in the dirt –
     this life has been fine

With Five Ranch Hands Remembering The Klamath

Four

Late spring in Klamath,
when snow runs like Rocky Road
ice cream from mountains,
        we'd fist gray granite
        to pelt the brown hides of deer
        and drive them – grunting –
                salt hungry – from camp,
                these memories go under my
                pillow while I sleep.

With Five Ranch Hands Remembering The Klamath

Five

I watched the brook trout
eye drowning horse flies, intent
on filling bellies,
    before stabbing pool
    with sunburnt arms to jerk them
    from concentric rings.
        It was a good meal
        to work for on Sunday nights.
        I'd laugh and give thanks.

Turning Sixty In Another's Spring

Gray clouds spit rain for three days over budding oak, maple and box elder along the Blue Earth River – Minnesota is still too cold and dry for dandelions to line dirt roads that stretch like branches to a yellow horizon. Black fields fold like bark over gnarled limbs. White ice melts from headstones in the Methodist cemetery, erodes frozen sod from fencepost, fills the ditch as it recedes like gums from enameled wood braced with barbed wire.

It was here, with mud-caked boots, under hours of six o'clock fog beside a steaming John Deere diesel I decided to die alone – to reject a son and his leather bola wrapped in green Christmas paper, refused to hop a stick shift Ford flatbed in clouds of gravel-gold dust as a daughter huffs, *does that sound right dad?*

Wind blows topsoil into my eyes, sticks to teeth and nostrils where car exhaust once tickled the back of my throat. It's been too long, too many Indian Summers spent in the cellar, too many moonless nights on vacant roads and too many ashes in the wood burning stove. . .

Find more online:

http://www.poetryinprint.com/

To contact friends of m otis aavenüe

email otis.aavenue@gmail.com

Look for these other great books by m otis aavenüe

1. Grasses of Nashville Township
2. PinMonkey

WHAT CRITICS HAVE SAID

The author must have the Devil in him. A Nashville, TN private university security guard and aspiring Southern Baptist hymn writer.

BOLD *and titillating as* Fear and Loathing in Las Vegas *found in a cheap motel restroom.* A community college double associates degree seeker in psychology and english.

I just like the writer. A homosexual hair stylist from Flagstaff, AZ.

Best poetry I have read in a long time. m otis aavenüe's mom.

Many of the poems in this chapbook have appeared online and in print in anthologies, magazines and university publications. Selected poems were included in the microdot media publication Grasses of Nashville Township.

Preserve m otis aavenüe's Work Fund:

One dollar from each book sold is dedicated the Preserve m otis aavenüe's Work Fund

www.ingramcontent.com/pod-product-compliance
Lightning Source LLC
Chambersburg PA
CBHW070802050426
42452CB00012B/2458